I0462132

Becoming
Frustration-Free
Utilizing Frustration to Benefit Business & Life

Greg Orth

Copyright © 2014 Greg Orth

All rights reserved.

ISBN-13: 978-1501016424

DEDICATION

For My Wife, Kathleen

CONTENTS

1   Discovering Frustration-Free   1

2   Constant Improvement   5

3   Facing Frustration   9

4   Utilizing Frustration   11

5   Becoming Frustration-Free   13

6   Maintaining a Frustration-Free Experience   19

7   New Applications for the Frustration-Free Process   21

1
DISCOVERING FRUSTRATION-FREE

In March of 2012, on a plane bound for California, I brought a small notebook that was a gift from my employer. The spiral bound, blank notebook was a perk, or swag, given out for winning their Kaizen of the Year Award. Kaizen is Japanese for "improvement", or "change for the better". This award is given annually to the team whose efficiency project saved the company the most money, or best demonstrated the innovative approach to solutions that they embraced.

The idea for the Kaizen project came to me after a frustrating day at work. My job in the department was titled "problem solver", and along with a few others, were tasked with handling orders that had problems. On that day, like most others, I was frequently interrupted by some small detail or another that prevented me from taking the next step in a simple task, on a standard problem during a typical day.

At the time, I remembered an old story, of a war that was lost due to a broken or missing cotter pin, or lubrication on a chariot wheel. The chariot's wheel fails, causing the defensive flank of the attack to collapse, and the war was lost, over a simple cotter pin on a single wheel.

At work, my "missing cotter pin" was a missing ink pen…or a tape gun, or supply of the correct labels, or any number of other small daily problems that had been with the company since its beginning, often causing me to call out "My kingdom for an ink pen!"

On this particular day, I mentally ridiculed the company as never before, wishing for a *single* day of processing without frustration, minor or major, and knowing that the other employees were like me, in simply wanting nothing more than a frustration-free day at work.

These small frustrations were experienced by all of the employees, and acted as sand in the gears of our process. Morale was low, and our department was unknowingly suffering a loss of productivity as a result.

With nearly 100 processors working a 10 hour shift, both day and night, I began to calculate the savings that we could gain by being better organized. If each person stopped loosing thirty minutes a day to small interruptions and frustrations, ones that could be solved through better supply management, it could make a real difference.

The common scenario went something like this: an employee needs a pen to fill out a standard form, leaves his desk to find one, and on the way, stops to ask a friend "What's up?" The brief gossip triggers his friend to then pass on the same gossip later, when they also leave the desk for something needed. Only to be repeated again, an hour later, when the first person runs out of the form he needed the pen for to begin with.

The supply of needed materials was unreliable, and there was no good system in place to prevent workers from running out of something several times a day. The problem grew with each new employee, costing the company more and more, and disrupting other departments downstream. As a result, morale suffered, cycle times were delayed, and mandatory overtime was often called simply to catch up, which raised frustration levels even further.

When I returned to work the following day, I presented a proposal to the Senior Operations Manager asking him to acknowledge the problems and do the simple things needed to reduce frustrations. Surprisingly, he listened and agreed, and the resulting Kaizen project focused on these problems.

A team was chosen, and tasked with eliminating clutter on the desks and solving the re-supply issues. We bought dispensers for the six different labels and seven different bags we used. Previously, all of these items were thrown in a box on our desks, resulting in constant clutter and frustration. The Kaizen project tackled these and other related challenges.

We created a better re-supply system for items used daily, but more importantly, developed a new approach to the underlying problems we faced. No longer would the company ignore "seemingly" minor supply issues.

The simple act of reducing clutter gave us more desk space, which improved productivity and allowed us to focus more on quality. These improvements, as hoped, boosted morale by greatly reducing frustration.

The results were better than expected, with $1.25 million saved the first year through increased productivity. But how could such a simple fix have such a large effect? Here's how: with wasted time and frustration reduced, the employees were able to process additional items per hour. For example, an increase of individual productivity, from 14 units per hour to 20 per hour, increase the total number of items processed during a ten hour shift. If we take 100 employees working for 10 hours, it gives us a total of 1,000 labor hours per shift. If each person currently produces 14 units per hour (UPH), multiplied by 1,000 labor hours per shift, we get 14,000 units processed per 10 hour shift.

With the improvements in place, we could increase productivity from 14 to 20 units per hour per person. We've now gone from 14,000 units per shift to 20,000 units, while using the same number of people and hours as before.

In other words, the company's "units per hour" and/or "cost per hour" improved. Let's translate this to dollars; if each employee cost the company twenty dollars per hour, (the *total* cost per person, per hour), and they process twenty units in one hour, this breaks down to 20 units for twenty dollars, or a cost of $1.00 per unit. If an employee only processes 14 per hour, as we previously had, not 20, the cost jumps to $1.42 per unit. This 42 cent difference per unit is enormous, and could make or break a company.

The Kaizen project succeeded in removing the sand from the gears of the process, and allowed for sharply increased productivity, but best of all, it reduced the frustration level of the employees. I was sold on a simple concept the moment it occurred to me; *seek out* frustration, and you will find opportunities for improvement.

I watched as the project's findings were incorporated into the other departments in the building, and to other buildings in the global network. This approach is now a key component in all process design, development and testing at the company's fulfillment centers worldwide.

The lessons I embraced as a result were two-fold; first, commit to eliminating frustration, and all will benefit, secondly, the quirky but true principle of constant improvement through constant improvement. I realized then that "frustration-free" had become a way of looking at things not only in my own life, but in the world as well.

4

2
CONSTANT IMPROVEMENT

Constant improvement, or in business speak, *continuous* improvement is a simple concept to understand, yet difficult to implement. The "improvement" component can easily be embraced by any business, employee, supervisor, associate or worker. Improvement is simply the process of solving problems, thus, as problems are solved, things improve.

For most companies, it's the word "continuous" that becomes the challenge. How many hard working employees have heard a version of the question; what have you done for me lately? A good manager or leader may have a track record of solving a problem, resolving a crisis, or coming up with a great new concept or idea, only to have these accomplishment forgotten when the pressure is on again to drive better results.

The ability to deliver ever improving results on a consistent basis is a rare talent, and those who have it are usually well paid. We all have seen promotions given to those who get results, solve problems, close deals, make sales, or satisfy customers. For the rest of us, we are left wondering what they have that we don't.

Is it education, training, IQ, or street smarts? Whatever it is, it's the difference between those who succeed, and those who don't. Many have spent thousands on education, hoping to one day "have it", to learn the secret to success, how to close a deal, solve a problem, achieve a goal, or earn a promotion. These desires all have something in common, they all reflect a desire for improvement.

Lucky for us humans, our DNA contains the desire for improvement. This desire was the driving force behind the American Revolution, as Colonists became evermore dissatisfied with government. The same desire fuels innovation in our homes, transportation, health care and workplace.

Without the desire for improvement, Henry Ford would never have replaced the Model T with the Model A, or any other model. Without this desire, we would still be hunting wild animals with hand-thrown spears, cutting them up with stone knives, and burning our fingers as we cooked over an open fire. Without the desire for improvement, a nation could easily be defeated by another nation that *did* improve, as primitive defenses would be no match for modern weapons.

Improvements have given us better cars and homes, healthcare and diets, schools, science, and ways to interact as a species. Improvement though, is also change, yet change is something humans fear and reject, and in doing so, we often reject improvement.

The internet, (an improvement) is filled with quotes about why we fear change. The reasons are rooted in our fear of the unknown. Our minds are reasonably comfortable facing the future if we believe it will be like the present, but if we believe that tomorrow will be *nothing* like today, our minds peer forward in time, only to find a void.

The greatest line of all, was delivered by President Franklin D. Roosevelt; "the only thing we have to fear, is fear itself."
Yet knowing that people fear change allows us to have compassion for those who suffer from it, including ourselves. Releasing the fear of change is only possible if we have some measure of control *over* it. This is the

difference between change happening *to* us, or *with* us.

Change happening *to* us is often unwelcomed, something to defend against, something to resist. This is hardwired in our DNA, a self-defense mechanism given by our creator. Conversely, change that happens *with* is welcomed in our lives, to solve problems, achieve goals, and give hope to future generations.

In business, Continuous Improvement, (CI) is the process of continuous change, and those in charge of it would be well served by including employees, associates and customers in the process. A smart business owner will allow employees to *own* the process of CI, because every employee simply wants their workday to be frustration-free.

A frustration-free workplace means that all tasks are achieved without resistance, problems, and delays. This is not our usual experience, at work or in the world.
How different it would be, as a customer, to have a frustration-free car buying experience, or trip to the mechanic. Imagine if you can, frustration-free home buying, or tax forms. These are tasks we dread because they are usually difficult and frustrating. But we can change that.

Greg Orth

3
FACING FRUSTRATION

Frustration, we all have it, experience it daily, tolerate it to some degree, and wish it would go away. At home, work, school and even at play, we all experience some form of frustration. Some of us hold it in as stress, others express it through complaints, while others curse, some even lash out, pounding their fist, or worse. Frustration can be felt consciously or subconsciously, acknowledged or ignored, faced directly, or denied.

In most companies, frustration is ignored, denied, and subconscious. It is something that the boss experiences, yet doesn't believe others do. It's something that the employees have, yet goes unnoticed by management. It's something that your customers are experiencing as they confront you, or the reason they inexplicably drop you entirely.

Even the most callus of companies that believe a frustrated employee is replaceable, realize that frustrated customers are not. Frustration is a corrosive, damaging morale, productivity, online reviews, and growth. In all of its forms, it is the sand in the gears of progress.

As an employee, how do we react to frustration? Do we try to ignore it, "share" it with co-workers, go through the chain of command, complain to HR, or go home and kick the dog? Do we ever verbalize these frustrations to those who can truly help? Unfortunately, most companies have no specific tools for resolving employee frustration.

As managers, leaders and owners, what do we do when presented with employee frustration? If we are like most, we listen politely, tell the frustrated person that they have "a valid point", and that their criticism "is fair", and "we'll look into it". Yet as soon as the person walks away, we grumble about having to deal with their complaints and criticism.

As leaders, do we listen to people long enough to truly hear their issue, or simply polarize against them, put up our shields and resent having our difficult day made even harder? How do we, as a business or company, handle employee frustration? Do we give it the respect it deserves, or ignore it, creating an environment perfect for organized unions?

Today, most medium and larger businesses have a separate department for handling employee problems; HR. Unfortunately, in too many companies, the HR department is there to deal with problem employees, not employees with problems, while some companies can't even tell the difference.

The result of ignored frustration is seen when workers "go postal" or sue an employer, or a boss fires a worker. In truth, the need for an HR department arose from the denial of frustration. The relationship between employee and employer, a business and its customers, or buyers and suppliers, are all subject to frustration, mostly ignored. But it need not remain so.

4
UTILIZING FRUSTRATION

Dare we look frustration in the eye and welcome it? The concept of utilizing frustration as a positive act is foreign to all of us, to leaders, owners, bosses and supervisors, it's foreign to us as workers, employees, and associates, to customers, vendors and buyers, and global business as we know it. This can change.

Frustration, the sand in the gears of our lives, can be removed. We can live a frustration free life, work in a frustration-free environment, and relate with each other in a frustration-free way. But we must change our attitude and approach to frustration, in the workplace, in our business dealings, in our communities and in our families. We must begin to see frustration as the blessing that it is; an opportunity for improvement.

In our ancient past, frustration with the spear was an opportunity for improvement. Frustration led to the invention of the wheel, the cart and wagon, the car, the airplane, the spaceship and beyond. From the abacus to the computer, it was frustration that led to improvement. The process can continue at an even greater speed if we accept and utilize frustration rather than resent it.

Utilizing frustration does not come naturally, but this can change. It can come about by better understanding and appreciating the role frustration can play in driving improvements in efficiency, quality, sales, customer and employee satisfaction, all leading to increased profits. If we overcome our fear of frustration, we open the doorway to insights, innovation, and improvements that were once obscured. If we actively *seek out* frustration and utilize it, we will break records!

Engagement with frustration can turn conflict into resolution, struggle into solution, it can turn the sand in the gears of business into the lubrication that keeps it running smoothly.

Embracing frustration is as simple as intentionally listening for it by inviting those in your company, your community, your family, even yourself, to express frustration in a positive and constructive environment, where it can be fully utilized.

This allows change without fear, to help us create a frustration-free workplace or process, website or employee, management team, supplier or customer.
By simply stating the *goal* of creating a frustration-free work environment, morale will improve, yet if we can deliver on this promise, the sky's the limit.

5
BECOMING FRUSTRATION-FREE

The process of becoming frustration-free is simple, but cannot be achieved by half-hearted efforts. Becoming frustration-free is both a goal and process, it's a goal that we set, and a process of continuous improvement.

Can a business, a process, a family or a person ever become truly frustration-free? Yes, if we address frustrations in the proper order, and put forth our full effort to resolve them. Then simply repeat.

With an ongoing, continuous effort to address top frustrations within a fixed period of time, we will experience consistently improving results.

Simply a commitment to becoming frustration-free can motivate business owners, managers, team leaders, employees, suppliers and vendors, to embrace continuous improvement as a guiding principle. The commitment can drive continuous improvements in morale, productivity, customer satisfaction and profit margin...and it can be done on a simple piece of paper.

Once the commitment is made to utilize frustration for improvement, we must determine which frustration is the top, or greatest one. This is done with a simple survey of those participating, the employees, managers, vendors, suppliers or customers.

The survey consists of three brief questions, with the answers being used to score or rate the frustration in terms of importance when compared to other frustrations in the group.

The three questions on the group survey are the following:

1- What is the main frustration you experience as one of our employees? (managers, vendors, customers, suppliers...etc.)

2- How often do you experience this frustration?
Several times: (per hour) (per day) (per week) (per month) (per year).

3- Please rate the frustration on a scale of 1-10, with 1 being the least frustrating, 10 the most frustrating.

This survey will give you the tools and data needed to determine which frustration is causing the greatest problem in the group.

Let's look closely at each question. The first one being "What is the main frustration you experience as one of our employees, managers, vendors, customers, suppliers...etc.?"

This question will allow us to determine which frustrations are the most common within the group, and by simply choosing the most common frustration, we are well on our way to improving the process and the human experience of that process.

There are some frustrations which many people experience, and some which only one person may experience, By choosing the most common frustration, we avoid the risk of going in the wrong direction, or "barking up the wrong tree", and *for now*, we will choose the one experienced by the most number of people. This will be the focus of the current project.

The second question, "How often do you experience this frustration? Several times (per hour) (per day) (per week) (per month) (per year)".

This question will allow the team to further rate the frustration by considering frequency. The more frequent the frustration, the more urgent a solution is needed.

Problems that are experienced several times per hour usually deserve the highest level of attention, and offer the greatest reward for our efforts. These frustrations, if addressed properly and solved, can quickly improve morale, productivity, and customer satisfaction.

Frustrations that occur less frequently can be just as frustrating or more so, yet their frequency places them on a different scale of importance. A weekly hard drive crash is extremely frustrating, yet an hourly one will mean that no work is possible at all, while an annual hard drive crash can be expected and planned for ahead of time.

When looking at the first and second question together, we can judge the importance of a minor frustration, such as changing an empty roll of labels once an hour, to a hard drive crash once an hour. It is easy to choose which frustration to focus on first; the hard drive crash.

We may discover that the second or third most common frustration happens to fewer people, but happens to them more frequently, thus it may become the top issue. A common weekly frustration may by passed by for a less common, hourly one. But making the *final* choice will require even more scrutiny.

Let's look then at the third question, "Please rate the frustration on a scale of 1-10, with 1 being the least frustrating, 10 the most frustrating."

This question allows us to rate the degree of importance of

a particular frustration to a particular person, job, task, or situation. For example, we may have lots of people who are frustrated by delays in the break room waiting for a microwave, but it may receive a low score in terms of how frustrating it is.

Let's compare for example someone who runs out of labels doing a task that uses 5 labels per hour to someone who runs out of labels during a task that requires 500 labels per hour. At 500 per hour, every second counts, and running out of labels even for a few minutes represents a serious amount of downtime, or may result in a bottleneck, requiring additional effort to handle.

Downtime and bottlenecks affect all downstream customers, both internally and externally, potentially costing an operation significant loss of productivity, profits, and customer satisfaction. It also becomes a frustration for the downstream customers, requiring even more resources to resolve.

Remember, when dealing with the survey results, keep in mind that some frustrations will come from something happening upstream of the frustration, yet impacting the downstream process.

The three questions in the survey allow us to determine what our most critical problem is, how frequently it occurs, and how much it impacts the ones directly experiencing it.

The results of the survey will guide us in the right direction as we plan the project which will implement solutions. The questions should steer us to the top frustration as determined by its frequency, severity and amount of people it impacts. There may be more than one frustration which seems to be "the worst", and it is the job of the team to select the one they feel will have the greatest impact.

For most companies, I recommend that the survey be given once a month, allowing thirty days to put together a team of problem solvers, choose the top frustration, and address the issue. Thirty days will pass by quickly, and we should not underestimate the need for adequate time when eliminating the top frustrations from a process.

The team of people selected to take on and resolve the frustration, should be a mixture of the ones experiencing the frustration, and those not experiencing it. The reason for this comes from the fact that when solutions are put in place, the ones who were experiencing the frustration will notice an instant improvement in the process, and may declare the project a smashing success.

The ones on the team that had never experienced the problem, will, for the first time, experience the new and improved process, and may find fault and frustration even in the new method.

The one who experienced the frustration on a regular basis may not be able to see anything beyond the frustration-free experience. By also having a different person experience the new process, we allow for the possibility that unintended frustrations were built into the new process.

The team of problem solvers assigned to tackle the "frustration-of-the-month" can and should use time tested problem solving techniques, such as the ones found in Kaizen, PDCA (plan, do, check, and adjust), Lean Manufacturing, Six Sigma and ISO 9000 Quality Management.

If there is no previous program for problem solving, then one of the above listed systems may work, be adapted, or we may simply create a team based on individual circumstance.

Some common tools available in these programs include flowcharts, which are graphic depictions of a process, drawn out step by step. Flowcharts allow us to see a complex process in smaller, step by step detail. Creating one will allow us to see where, in a process, the frustration occurs. It also keeps the project in focus, acting to ground the problem in tangible terms, defined and clear to all.

Flow charts can focus on either the macro or micro view, for example, a car dealership can focus on a frustration found in the car buying process overall, or a single frustration found in one step of the loan approval process. The method used to address the top frustration is of less importance than the fact that we identify the target correctly.

The cause of most frustrations fall into one of four categories, known commonly as 4M; Material, Method, Man, Machine, and examining a frustration's relationship to these four categories will help reveal the root cause.

Many frustrations can be resolved by simply being better organized, and for this, we can turn to a method called 5S, or Sort, Straighten, Shine, Standardize, and Sustain. When frustrations are caused by disorganization, 5S guides us to sort out what's needed, arrange it logically, clean the area, make this the new standard, and maintain it.

Another common tool used to analyze a problem or frustration is the "5 Why's" approach. Using this method, we would take the top frustration, and ask "Why do we have this frustration?" The answer will be tested again with a second "Why". By asking "why?" enough times, we work through layers to find the root cause.

Let's look at an example. If the frustration comes from a conveyor line that frequently jams, we would ask "why". The first "why" might reveal that the boxes on the line turn slightly as they travel, causing the crooked ones to jam. The second "why" reveals that the conveyor's photo-eye feature stops and starts the line as intended, but also causes the boxes to turn slightly with each stop. The third "why" reveals that the boxes turn because the line was designed for wider boxes, and the excess width allows the boxes to turn. "Why" they turn is simply because they *can*, and that by adding a pair of guide rails to the narrow the conveyor, the frustration can be solved.

Another helpful tool in solving the root cause of a frustration is the "Cause and Effect" or "fishbone" diagram, which, like "mind-mapping" is ideal for brainstorming in a group. Mapping out a problem with a group is critical to solving it. Each additional brain in a brainstorming session is a tool to help root cause a problem, so it's good to have at least three people in any session. Be aware, larger groups are often better, yet take longer to work with, thus 15 people would not likely be needed to solve the jammed conveyor line, but may be needed when a problem impacts several departments and hundreds of people.

There are additional tools found in Kaizen, Lean Manufacturing, Six Sigma, and ISO 9000 that can be used by most any company, and countless books available on their use and benefits, but how do we choose one?

Problem solving a quality issue, especially in manufacturing, may be best served by Six Sigma, while a complex assembly line, process, or multiple departments operating together, may benefit from Lean Manufacturing and the Kaizen approach, while basic mind-mapping is well suited for working groups, an individual, family, or community.

The magic of the frustration-free approach lies not only in its ability to help us solve problems, but in its ability to do so in a way that is user friendly and versatile. The process is not designed to address "blanket" frustrations; my pay, my boss, my co-workers, rather, it's designed to help with things that do not function as they should; a process, a machine, a design, a layout, a method.

The talent exists in any group to successfully solve problems once they are correctly identified. We simply need to use these tools to pinpoint and solve a problem, and repeat the process monthly.

If we are willing, we can drive continuous improvement, create a frustration-free environment, build morale, and increase our bottom line, …twelve times a year!

6
MAINTAINING FRUSTRATION-FREE

Having initiated the frustration-free approach, we have a few things to keep in mind. The process does not run automatically, and though we may have seen dramatic improvements in productivity, morale, quality and safety, we cannot rest. The rewards of continuous improvement will soon dry up if we celebrate our early successes and falsely believe that the process has done its job and is no longer needed.

The secret to the success of this method lies not simply in its ability to deliver solutions to the most obvious problems, but to the least obvious ones. In business, it is far easier to spot the double-handling of product, a chronic bottleneck, or the un-necessary distance between the components of an assembly line, than the least obvious frustrations, such as slight variations in a method or process that can be so elusive, so difficult to discover, and yet so gratifying when resolved.

Only by following the program's monthly format, will the most glaring frustrations dissolve to reveal the more subtle ones beneath, the ones that may not have been recognized at the start, or scored so low in the survey as to not yet be a priority. Yet month by month, ever smaller frustrations work their way to the top of the list, and signal an opportunity to gain that last few degrees of improvement that are nearly impossible to capture with other approaches.

For an example, let's look back in time to the last used car we purchased. If it had a dead battery or a flat tire when we bought it, we gave that immediate attention and made the repair, and went from having a car that would not start or move, to one that would. That was a dramatic improvement, but it would not be the last. As we drove the car, we may have noticed that one headlight was out, and it shifted poorly, jerking between gears. Once those repairs were handled, we may have noticed that the engine has a faint knocking sound, and by now, we discover that the gas mileage is lousy. Back to the mechanic.

Once the third round of repairs was complete, we may have noticed that the muffler was somewhat louder than it should be, and that the seat leans a little to the right at an uncomfortable angle, and by the way, the left front stereo speaker has a buzz.

As we deal with the greatest problems first, the flat tire and the dead battery, the lesser problems become noticeable. We would have never noticed the buzzing speaker with a dead battery, or over the noise of a muffler and an engine knock.

Having solved the most important problems, the more obscure ones can then be discovered and resolved.
Did this mean that the car was still as bad as the day we bought it? No, it was constantly improving, it was becoming more dependable and reliant, smoother running and more pleasant to drive, and eventually, the gas mileage became better than expected.

Would we have replaced the buzzing speaker before fixing the flat tire and changing the battery? No. Will we eventually get around to the lightly stained carpet and the small tear in the seat? Yes, but not on the first day.

It is a process of continuous improvement, a process, not a single event accomplished at once. To have the fine car we desire, or the frustration-free experience we long for, we must follow the process, and trust in the outcome.

The month-by-month format for becoming frustration-free is designed to discover those small frustrations that were overlooked amidst the noise and disruption of the larger problems. This is how we gain the final increments of improvement long after other methods have stopped delivering. This is how we create and maintain a frustration-free experience.

Greg Orth

7
NEW USES FOR THE FRUSTRATION-FREE PROCESS

The process of becoming frustration-free can be used by individuals as well as groups. For an individual, we would simply list our top 10 frustrations for example, and use the same three questions to evaluate them. Once evaluated, we brainstorm and problem solve. This can and will be an individual creative act, one that tests our ability to think outside the box.

Once the top frustration is known, we can call on any internal and external resources we have, or seek out new ones. Brainstorming will pay off, as we each hold the keys to our own happiness inside. Even if we have help, it is up to each individual to see it through, and repeat the exercise monthly.

For individuals, bear in mind, solutions to a frustration should not rely on other people changing their "ways" to make your life better. Changing the way a household operates is like changing the way a factory operates, a better plan must be created, agreed upon, followed and maintained. It never works to simply tell someone, "Don't be a slob", but rather, look to solutions that fit your needs for organization and solve problems that the household shares in common. Simply solving your frustration by creating one for another family member solves nothing. A truly frustration-free household means that all occupants feel respected throughout the process and with solutions.

As we have seen, the only way to eliminate frustration is to utilize it. In doing so, we can improve our homes, our assembly lines and manufacturing plants, our service centers, and our public and private institutions.

The process of becoming frustration-free works as well for a large .com business as it does for a small daycare. A steel mill can increase profits by the same percentage as an auto dealership. An automotive plant can see the same improvement in productivity as a grocery chain, and a school system can have the same level of morale improvement as a textile mill.

In today's world, frustration is found in every part of our lives, in every industry, sector, sale, purchase and customer return. Frustration is found in your company's fulfilment centers and reverse logistics systems, and any place where people come together to achieve a goal. Becoming Frustration-Free can work anywhere creative people are frustrated, thus, the U.S. Military can gain as much as Toyota, Ford, General Motors, and John Deere.

From mechanics to farmers, the frustrations we face limit what we can accomplish in a day, they limit what a welder or a lumberjack can achieve, what a chef can produce, and a dishwasher can clean, what a teacher can teach, and a student can learn.

Morale problems are found in both the sanitation and banking industry, in law enforcement and film production, in prisons and resort hotels.

We can utilize frustration anywhere in the world while doing any task imaginable. Frustration, as a tool for driving improvement, works for professionals, amateurs, men, women and children, and will improve our workplace, home life, and recreation time.

If we are willing to embrace and utilize frustration, the sky is the limit!

ABOUT THE AUTHOR

Greg Orth, author of "Becoming Frustration-Free", is an inventor and award winning problem solver. Hired by a major e-commerce company, his leadership skills were put to use in its fast paced, growth environment, where he learned the problem solving methods of Six Sigma, Lean Manufacturing, and Kaizen. He has worked on numerous efficiency projects and supervised departments of up to 80 employees.

The author's discovery of the secret benefits of frustration led to his surprisingly simple approach to solving a wide variety of problems at work and home. Greg is convinced that the full potential for using Six Sigma, Lean Manufacturing, and Kaizen to improve our lives is still in its infancy, and has applied these tools to the task of creating good government in his upcoming book, "We, The Third Party".

www.ingramcontent.com/pod-product-compliance
Lightning Source LLC
Chambersburg PA
CBHW021417170526
45164CB00002B/689

* 9 7 8 1 5 0 1 0 1 6 4 2 4 *